Japanese Stencil Designs

One Hundred Outstanding Examples

Collected and Introduced by

Andrew W. Tuer, F.S.A.

Dover Publications, Inc., New York

Published in Canada by General Publishing Company, Ltd., 30 Lesmill Road, Don Mills, Toronto, Ontario.

Published in the United Kingdom by Constable and Company, Ltd., 10 Orange Street, London WC2H 7EG.

This Dover edition, first published in 1967, is a republication of the work originally published *circa* 1892 under the title *The Book of Delightful and Strange Designs, Being One Hundred Facsimile Illustrations of the Art of the Japanese Stencil-Cutter.*

The Introductory Essay appeared in French and German as well as in English in the original edition.

DOVER *Pictorial Archive* SERIES

International Standard Book Number: 0-486-21811-2
Library of Congress Catalog Card Number: 67-19699

Manufactured in the United States of America
Dover Publications, Inc.
180 Varick Street
New York, N.Y. 10014

THE BOOK OF DELIGHTFUL AND STRANGE
DESIGNS BEING ONE HUNDRED FACSIMILE IL-
LUSTRATIONS OF THE ART OF THE JAPANESE
STENCIL-CUTTER TO WHICH THE GENTLE
READER IS INTRODUCED BY ONE ANDREW
W. TUER, F.S.A. WHO KNOWS NOTHING
AT ALL ABOUT IT.

LONDON :
The Leadenhall Press, Ltd : 50, Leadenhall Street, E.C.

Liberty & Co., London, Paris, and Yokohama.

Simpkin, Marshall, Hamilton, Kent & Co., Ltd :

NEW YORK : Charles Scribner's Sons, 743 & 745, Broadway.

PARIS :
Baudry et Cie., 15, rue des Saints-Pères.

LEIPZIG :
F. A. Brockhaus, 16, Querstrasse.

dedicated

to that

most capricious

never-to-be-understood

weathercocky

provokingly incorruptible

and

absolutely necessary

person

the gentle reader

Introductory

*W*e are not lucky people as a rule, Gentle Reader, you and I, but the good things and the pretty things of this life—which seem to be pitched about in a haphazard sort of way—must fall into someone's lap, and our turn has come.

The treasure, whereof we are content to share the strange and fascinating beauties, is apparently of little account. Merely some sheets of pierced brown paper. We will imagine for a moment that the white portions forming the designs in the facsimile illustrations shewn herein are cut entirely away, and that the backs are of the same dark hue as the fronts: they are now to all intents and purposes real Japanese stencil plates.

We already know, you and I, that impressions from these stencil plates are used in decorating the cotton or crêpe so largely used in the dress of the Japanese of both sexes. We know intuitively that in transferring or printing, the Japanese stenciller must use a large soft brush giving readily to the slightest pressure, otherwise his frail stencils would soon be torn to pieces ; and we feel certain that he charges his brush with a sufficient quantity of pigment to give a full impression but not sufficient to get under the edges and blur the sharpness of the design.

Certain peculiarities are noted. For instance, each plate has at top or bottom two small punctures which form no part of the design ; these we see at once are "register" marks. In actual use by the Japanese workman, a pin or point is passed through each of these two holes and into the corresponding marks left by the previous impression ; in this way perfect "register" (fitting) and continuity in the printing of the design are ensured. At home, the lithographic printer "registers" his work very much in the same way.

Some of the designs, we note, are complete in themselves (see No. 26) and others are incomplete, or rather can be made complete only by continuous printing. No. 7 is an example incomplete not only at top and bottom but at the sides also, so that it can be repeated at discretion either way, according to the width of the material worked upon. In printing the broad way of the design, the stencil is simply

moved onward so that the lower part is registered on to the upper part of the impression last made ; but to get a continuous design the narrow way, it is necessary to turn the stencil plate right over and print from the reverse side. Reductions of design No. 7 are shewn here treated in both ways.

As the thrifty children of the Luminous Land waste nothing, it causes no surprise to find that their stencil plates are mostly made of disused documents.

It was observed that some of the stencils have curious little devices (see No. 37) nicked in the margins, which must mean something or they would not be there, and it was soon discovered that each had its fellow bearing the same device. These turned out to be pairs for printing in two colours, part of the design being cut out on one plate and part on the other. A great many of the best and most beautiful designs, however, we found to bear no such marks, and these single plates are obviously intended for one printing only. It is principally these single plates, complete in themselves, that figure herein. And we thought that a book of Japanese stencil plates themselves would be more acceptable than direct impressions from them. Later, it was noticed that some few of the designs are divided amongst three or more plates and require that number of separate printings to complete them. Owing to this splitting up or dividing, stencil plates prepared for multiple colour-printing naturally have a weak and uninteresting appearance.

We came to the conclusion that our collection, part of which had already been secured for the South Kensington Museum, probably formed a portion of the stock-in-trade of a professional Japanese stenciller. Many of the plates have seen much wear. On some of those where the design is distributed over several, the pigments have been left by the Japanese artist, shewing exactly what colours were last used.

Stencil plates can hardly be a publicly marketable commodity in Japan any more than holed loom-cards or engraved wooden blocks are publicly marketable at home : they simply form part of the working tools, or material, of the printer or decorator of cotton goods. It is surmised that the collection was sent to this country by some European who was struck by the marvellous beauty of the designs and the wonderful skill displayed in the cutting out. The person who sent over our plates was not the first European to discover the beauty of the Japanese stencil, for every now and then new and unused plates, but of feeble and conventional design, find their way over here for sale. These, however, like a certain notorious person's razors, seem to be made to sell, and they form a percentage, hardly appreciable, of the ship-loads of Japanese fans and pans moulded in millions to one pattern for the European market.

The Gentle Reader points out that the designs of some few of our stencils seem to have a strangely familiar look, but, on a somewhat closer

examination, the imitations of printed inscriptions forming them are found to be quite meaningless. Many of the letters are reversed or upside down, and groups of the same letters are so ingeniously placed that for some time it was not discovered that the plate is filled with mere repetitions. Some of the "inscriptions" are composed of monograms repeated over and over again, and probably the complacent man who walks about clad in raiment covered with symbols which he knows cannot be deciphered by himself or anyone else feels a very superior person indeed. No doubt these letters and monograms were borrowed from the Portuguese and Dutch traders in the sixteenth and seventeenth centuries when they first visited Japan.

Background patterns, which it would only be a waste of space to shew full size, sometimes have a bolder design stencilled over them by a second printing.

It is not so very long ago (1852) that the British Government paid a handsome reward—£4,000—to the fortunate individual who discovered

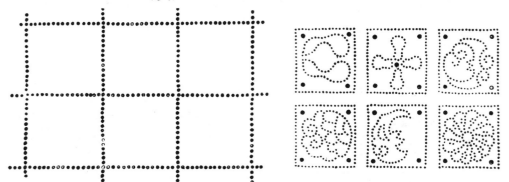

how to separate postage stamps by surrounding each one with a pin-hole border, and it provokes a smile to find a Japanese stencil plate divided into pin-hole squares. Here, however, the punctured holes are not intended as a means of separating but for stencilling a dotted border on to an arrangement of seals of the Daimios or territorial nobles—the seals in one colour and the border in another. The stencil plate with this punctured border is dated in Japanese characters 1825.

A curious stencil here reproduced in miniature is a letter from a lover to his lass. It will be noticed that a certain symmetry is obtained

by the text being written at different angles. A most intelligent Japanese, Mr. Kataoka, says that this letter formed an important link in the evidence pertaining to an historical trial in which the lover and his lass were at loggerheads.   For decorative purposes this design requires two printings to complete it, a flowing and graceful daisy pattern from a second plate filling in the spaces between the writing.

Another love letter—that with the umbrella at side—reads:

Kara ka sa no
   honé no kazu hado
Otokowa aré dó
   hiro gêté sasuwa
     nushi bakari.

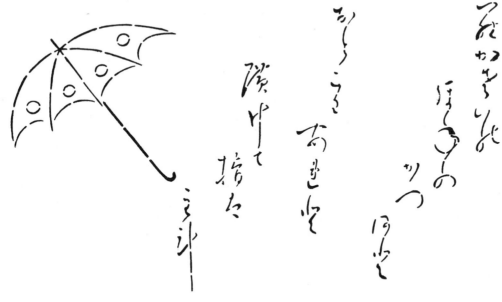

which in his quaintly terse English Mr. Kataoka translates—

> There are many admirers
> as limbs of parasol
> To you alone
> I open my heart.

and Mr. Wilfrid Meynell has versified:

> As parasols have many ribs
> So have I lovers—and their fibs.
> But only, only to your eye
> Is bared my heart and all it holds,
> Even as the parasol unfolds
> Beneath the burning sky.

Through necessary cutting away, some of the finer or more delicately designed stencils are so fragile that there is not enough paper left to hold them together. These are strengthened by the addition of silk threads stretched at regular intervals from top to bottom and from side to side. The threads are so fine that the stencil brush ignores them and they leave no mark; and the mesh or net they form is so strong, and withal so delicate, that a spider might have woven it. Its apparent irregularity in some of the examples shewn—shewn of set purpose—is due entirely to much wear.

The puzzling question arises : How did these threads get there ?

As they are incorporated with the substance of the paper, we feel instinctively that in cutting out the design, the workman, however skilled, could not have avoided severing them. The nut seemed uncrackable till some very fine parallel marks were noticed in the blank margins of the stencil plates corresponding to the threads running through the designs. This shewed that the threads were inside the structure of the paper, and as they obviously could not have been inserted edgeways with a needle, the elucidation pointed to a double thickness of paper. The difficulty, however, attending the production of a double stencil plate prepared in this manner is so enormous that for many, many days you and I, Gentle Reader, hesitated to credit what your common sense— I own to being the pigheaded one—pointed out as the only solution. With some little trouble we eventually split a stencil in two and found therein the threads snugly ensconced.

The question then narrowed itself to this :—

(1) How could a workman, unless endowed with a magician's skill, cut out two separate stencil plates of elaborate design exactly alike ?

(2) How did he get the threads into position? And, most difficult of all,

(3) How, after doing so, did he manage to cement the second
plate on to the first so that not only every thread is in exact
position, but the two pieces of paper have become prac-
tically one?

The explanation which follows can be believed only when it is
borne in mind what the Japanese are capable of doing with their fingers.

The artist-workman takes some half-dozen sheets of tough paper
made of mulberry fibre (*Broussonetia papyrifera*) prepared with the
juice of persimmon and waterproofed with a hard-drying oil. On the
top he places the artist's design drawn with ink. The sheets firmly
secured, he begins cutting with a long thin knife which he pushes before
him in the same way as a copperplate engraver at home uses the burin.
Slowly and accurately the keen blade cuts through the little pile of
paper following the curves of the design. Where there are punctured
holes or dots the knife is superseded by a fine punch, for if pins
were used a bur would be formed and the design would not print

clean and sharp. When the cutting out is finished, two of the sheets are damped so that they may expand and—what is of equal importance—contract equally in drying. One is laid down flat and covered with adhesive material. The threads are then one by one put in position, the ends sticking on to the margins. The second stencil is accurately laid over the first by means of upright pins placed in the "register" holes already mentioned, the two paper-plates are brought exactly together and the threads securely imprisoned. The joining of the two plates enclosing the threads is so absolutely perfect that a strong glass fails to disclose any sign of overlapping or unevenness. That anyone but a Japanese could execute such difficult work as this is simply impossible.

When the stencil-cutter has got through his first pile, he puts a stencilled impression on the top of the next as a guide in lieu of the original drawing which now has no independent existence, and he will continue cutting out the same design until he has a number sufficient for his purpose. From its nature, especially when the design is delicate and finely cut, a paper stencil plate cannot last very long. Many of the examples in our collection have seen so much service that they cannot again be used.

The Japanese stenciller produces two effects from a single plate : an impression in colour (indigo blue is largely used) on a white ground, and a white impression on a coloured ground. The former is by direct impression, and the latter by the impression being printed in what is termed "resist," a pigment or substance of which rice paste is the basis, that protects fabrics from the action of dyes. After the "resist" has been applied the fabric is dipped in a dye vat, and the "resist" is cleared away by washing.

A population of something like one-and-forty millions takes some dressing. The costume of the males—who in this perverse nation exceed the females by about half a million—consists of a loose robe from neck to feet gathered in at the waist and fastened with a girdle. The Japanese gentleman arrays himself in silk; the middle and lower classes in cotton and crêpe. The cotton socks usually worn are divided at the great toe, and the foot, when the loose slippers or pattens are kicked off, is freely used by the Japanese workman as a useful auxiliary to the hand.

In a series of papers, as valuable as they are interesting, on Japanese Life and Art, Mrs. Ernest Hart describes the costume of the Japanese woman, which she tells us consists principally of a long loose garment with wide open sleeves, known as a kimono, set high behind, cut low in front, folded across the chest and brought closely round the hips, and kept in position by a broad stiff sash called an obi. The Japanese women are extremely particular about the decoration of the kimono, which even in the cheapest descriptions of cotton or crêpe is stencilled with ever-varying designs wherein the prolific imagination of the artist runs riot. Mrs. Hart opines that "any cotton printer accustomed to the methods in use in England cannot fail to wonder at the elaborate designs he sees printed here on even the cheapest materials. The bold freehand drawing or the sketchy impressionism of the design, its complication, and the number of colours and shades introduced, make him realise at once that no blocks or rollers could give such results," an opinion the Gentle Reader and I are not slow in endorsing.

Many of our brown-paper treasures are too large to put into book form. Mrs. Ernest Hart possesses some extremely beautiful examples still larger, which she has been urged to frame decoratively with a sheet of white or tinted paper behind to throw up the designs. Thus treated, they would be sure to provoke much admiring comment, and might well find an abiding place on her walls.

The Japanese, who has naturally a fine sense of colour and form, is taught draftsmanship and painting in the same manner as he is taught writing—that is, copies are "set" which are laboriously transcribed over and over again until the pupil can draw, say, a chrysanthemum of conventional shape, almost as easily as you and I, Gentle Reader, can scribble *a b c*. The conventional treatment of objects, animate and inanimate, originally copied from the unimaginative Chinese, has been handed down from generation to generation. Attempts have certainly been made to discard this crippling cloak of conventionality, but with what success cannot here be fitly discussed. The one advantage—if it be an advantage—of their circumscribed art is freedom and quickness of manipulation, and while a Japanese drawing may too often be conventional, some of us at home could take a lesson from its harmonious colouring and delicate gradation of tones and be the better for it.

Professor Anderson tells us, in his scholarly and valuable mono-

graph on the " Pictorial Arts of Japan," that the introduction of the
stencil plate into Japan is attributed to a dyer, named Someya Yuzen,
towards the latter part of the seventeenth century, and that stencilling
has since been extensively employed in the decoration of Japanese
textile fabrics. It has also been occasionally used for the production of
hanging kakémonos (Japanese pictures) of an elaborate polychromatic
character. Kakémonos prepared in this way are now rarely to be met
with, but two specimens belonging to the early part of the present
century are in the British Museum collection, Nos. 3521-2.

It may be, however, that amongst the fine kakémonos belonging
to such studious collectors as Mr. W. C. Alexander, Mr. Ernest Hart,
Mr. Marcus B. Huish, Mr. Phené Spiers, and others, there are examples
difficult—perhaps impossible—to detect, of dual work begun with the
stencil plate and finished with the brush.

Professor Anderson has shewn us a very beautiful picture of a
hawk and wild goose on silk, apparently in water colours, but we are
assured that nearly the whole of the work is from stencil plates, the
colours being gradated before they are dry by skilful touches of the

artist's thumb or other part of the hand, which give to the half-tones the effect of delicate stippling. The pencil or brush is actually used in giving a few final touches after the removal of the last stencil plate. Pictures prepared in this way on squares of crêpe or silk are generally finished with delicate embroidery in coloured silks and metallic threads, and are often mounted in albums and sold as hand paintings.

The Gentle Reader says that we should number our stencils and say a word about them. The numbering is good, but I am afraid that "a word" means separate descriptions. Many—perhaps most—of the stencils are pregnant with meaning, and illustrate or suggest legends and superstitions either borrowed from the Chinese or having their origin in the dim mists of Japanese antiquity. To set forth these legends and stories in detail this book would have to be all introduction and no pictures. The Gentle Reader being pleasantly insistent, matters may be compromised by resorting to the sketchy manner of the auctioneer's catalogue :—

No. 1 is a design of chrysanthemums and butterflies ; 2, hare and waves ; 3, carp and waves or cataract ; 4, wild geese ; 5, chrysanthemums on moire antique ground ; 6, chrysanthemums and maple leaves ; 7, chrysanthemums, highly conventionalised ; 8, umbrellas with characters and crests of owners ; 9, bamboos conventionalised ; 10, rakes, brooms and fir branches (signs of longevity) ; 11, chrysanthemums and willow ; 12, crayfish ; 13, tortoise and waves ; 14, hairy-tailed tortoise (hairy tail, special mark of longevity) ; 15, cranes in bamboos ; 16, splashed design ; 17, carp and cataract ; 18, chrysanthemums with conventional chrysanthemum background ; 19, design of blossom and butterflies ; 20, chrysanthemums on ground suggested by gold spotted lacquer ware ; 21, phœnix on background of coarse threads suggesting weaving ; 22, varieties of chrysanthemums ; 23, chrysanthemums ; 24, fans with chrysanthemums and butterflies on spotted ground ; 25, "Ogi" fan with chrysanthemums and butterflies ; 26, carp and cataract ; 27, butterflies and bamboos ; 28, flower-baskets and creeping plants ; 29, grapes and vine leaves on a lined background ; 30, conventionalised flowers ; 31, cranes with highly conventionalised pines (sign of longevity) ; 32, design suggested by coarse matting ; 33, conventional dancers ; 34, conventional floral design with rays of light ; 35, gladioli on a highly conventionalised background of dew or water-drops ; 36, bamboo ; 37, maple leaves and waves (referred to in one of the " Hundred Poems ") ; 38, conventional peony ; 39, dragon and clouds in dotted outlines ; 40, carp and waves.

So much for the complete designs. In regard to the others where the subjects are repeated in the same illustration, we find fir cones, snails, fans, cobwebs, lattice-work, creepers, geometric figures, basket-work, grotesque figures, tigers, fishes, emblems, hawthorn pattern, dragons, peacocks' feathers, wild geese, flights of cranes, shells, diaper, cherry and plum blossom, grape vine, waves, water, ducks, aquatic plants, vases and gourds. The curious stencil No. 100 represents clappers used to frighten away birds ; and 102, which looks like a series of children's toys, really represents precious objects emblematic of good fortune, and known as takara-mono. Some of us may remember to have seen these emblems or marks on porcelain and lacquer ware, but their significance, even by the educated Japanese, appears to be little understood.

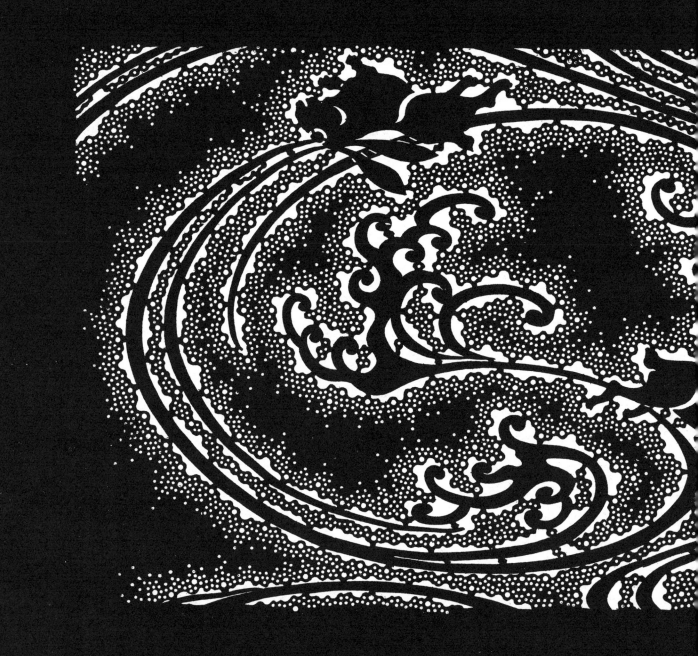

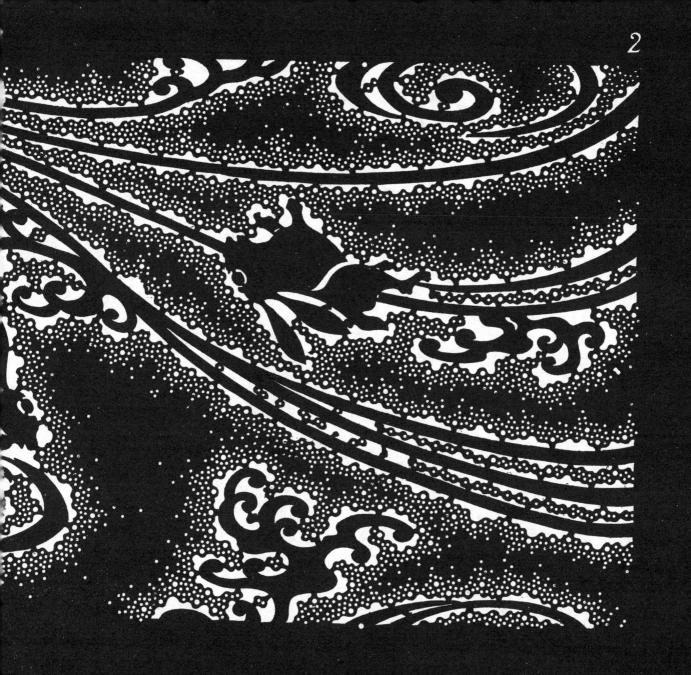

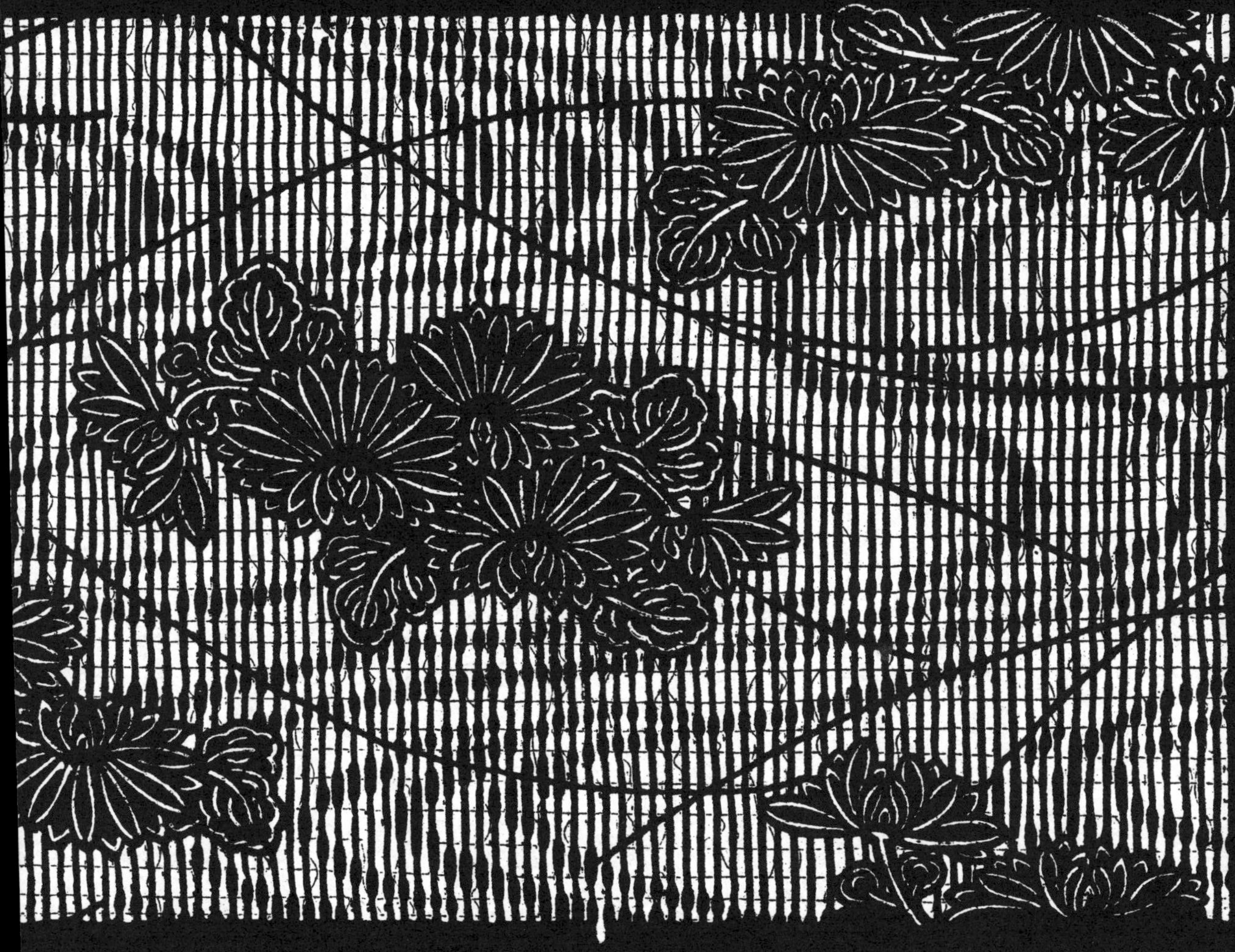

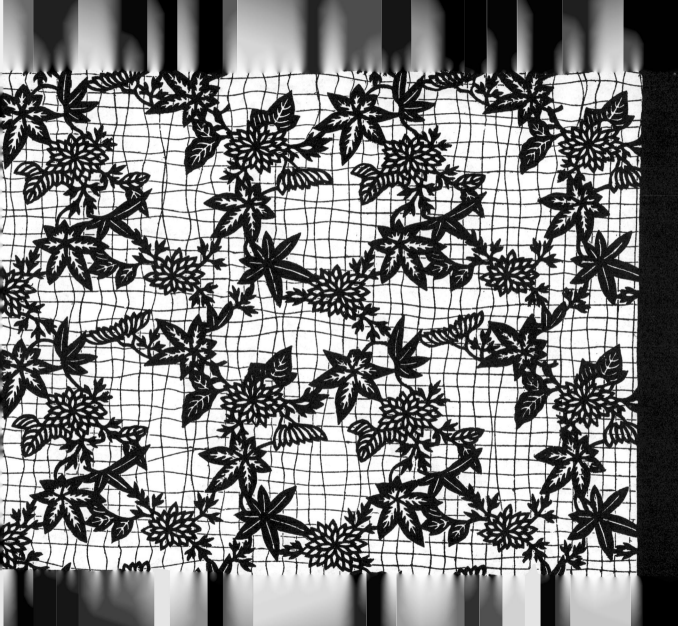

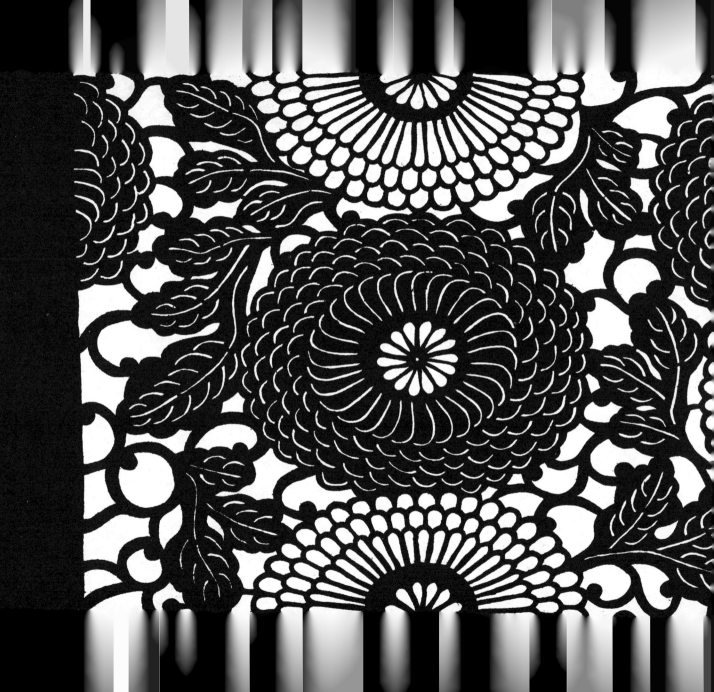

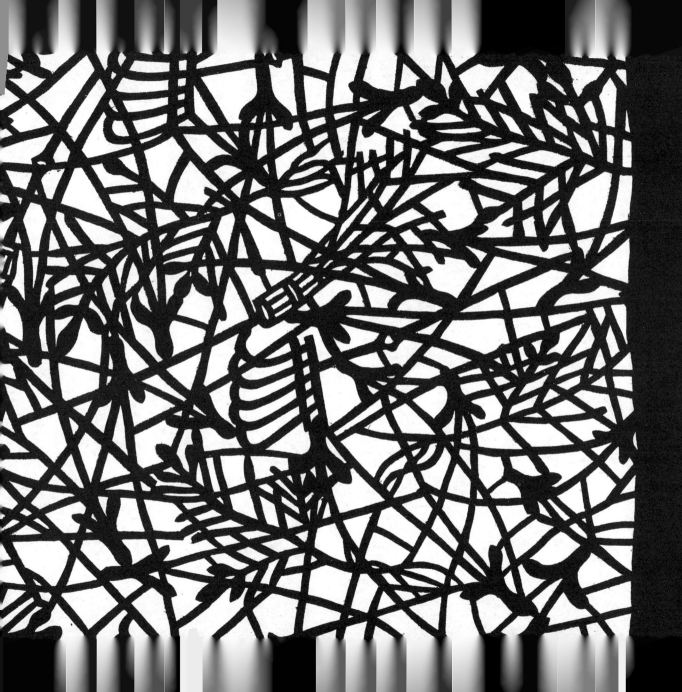

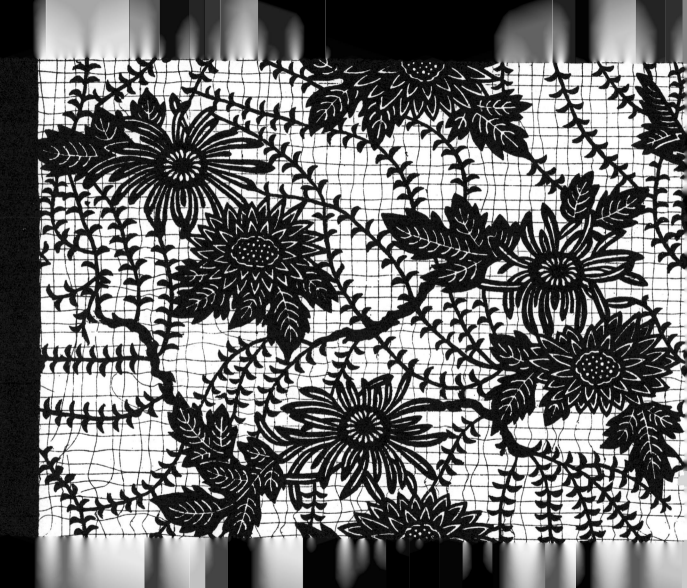

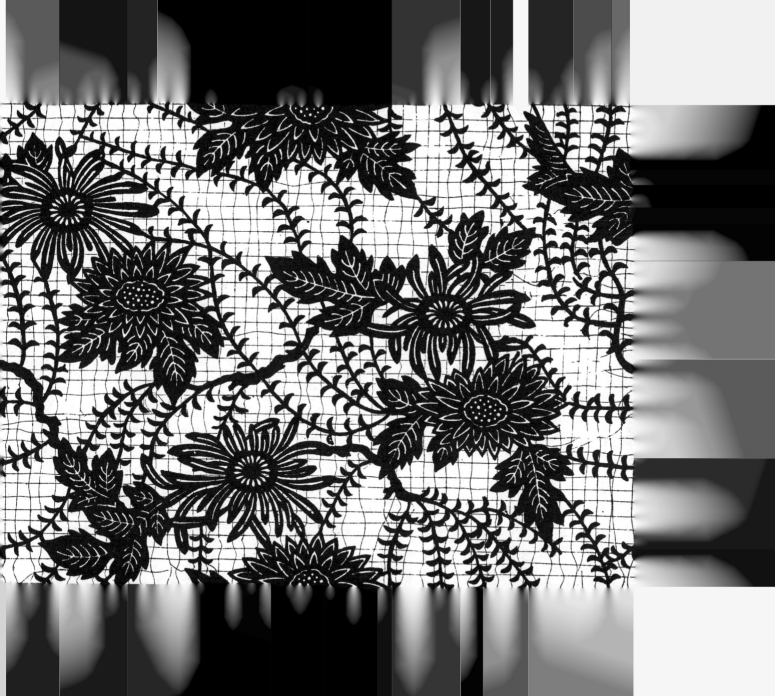

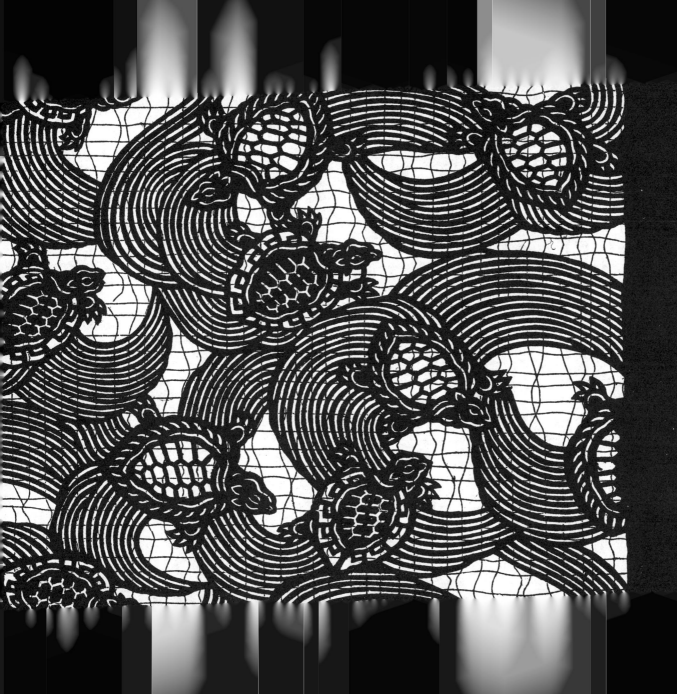

18

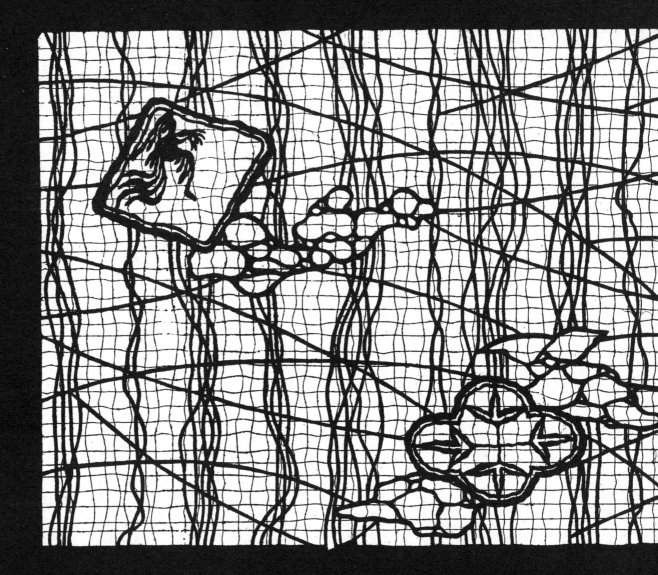

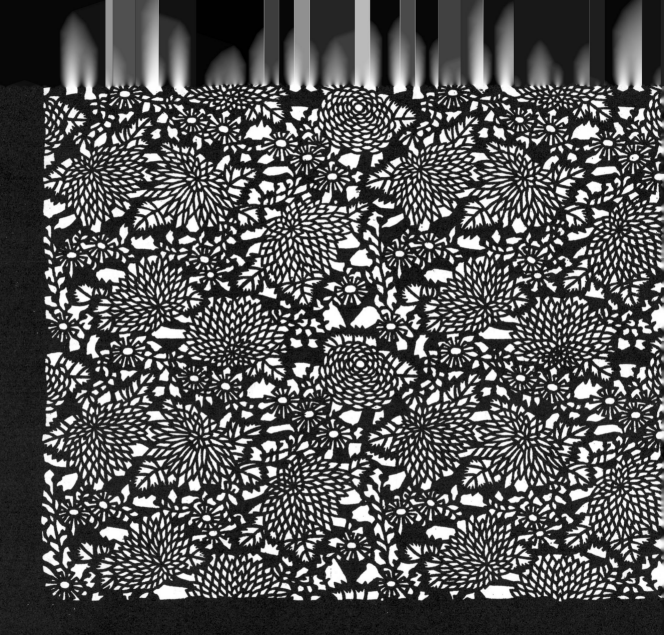

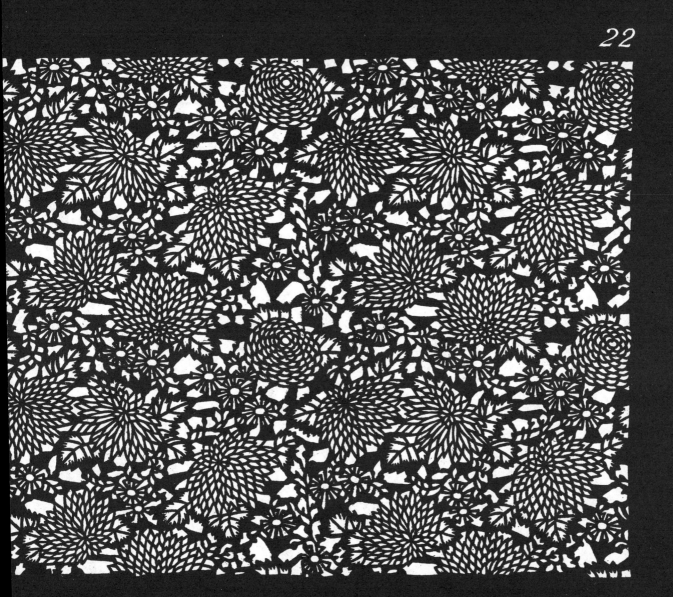

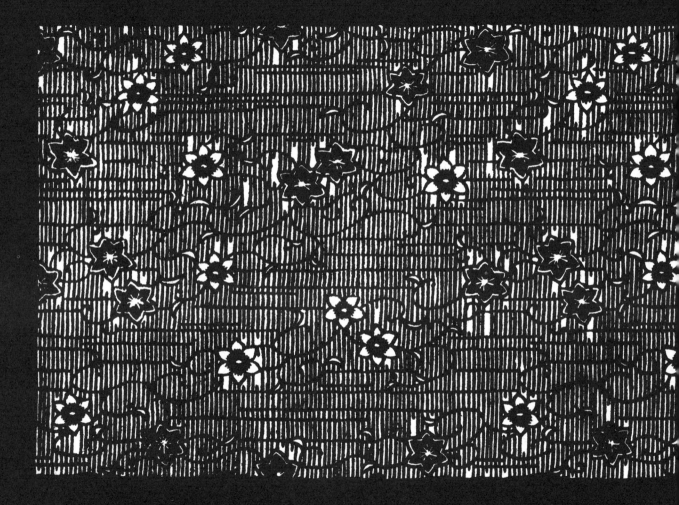

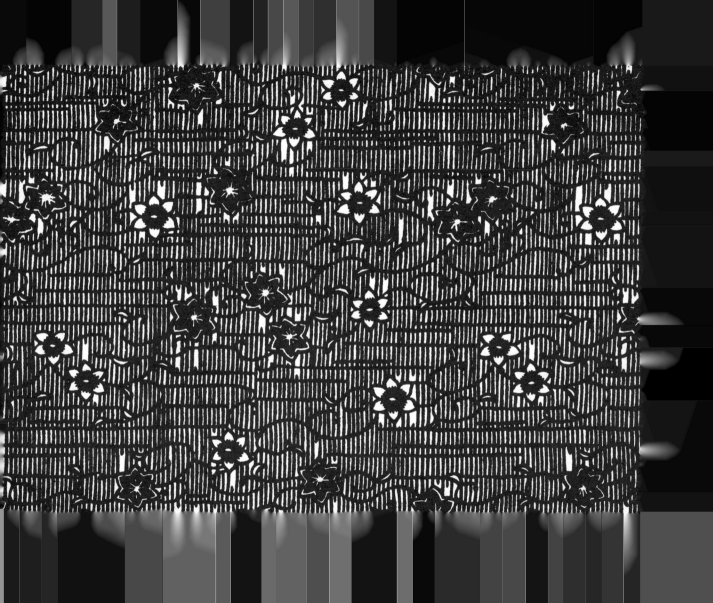

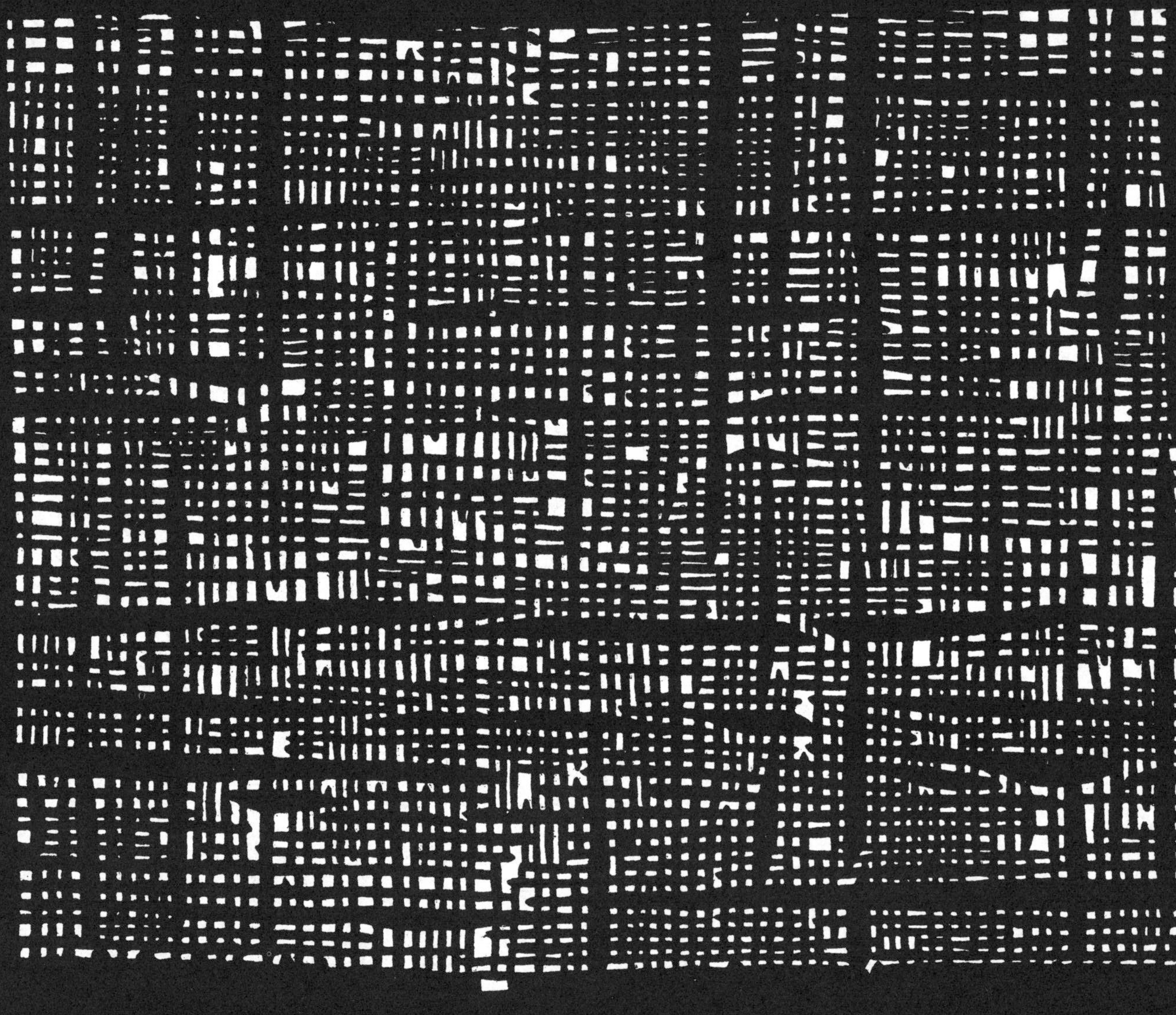

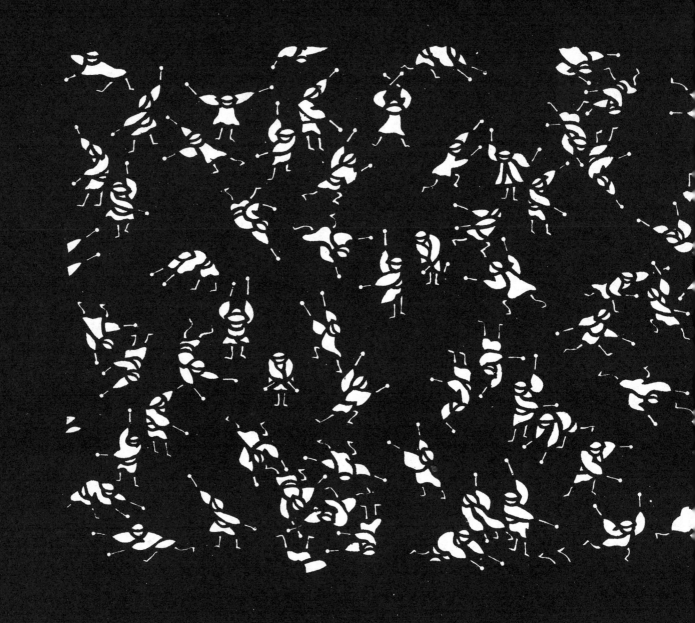

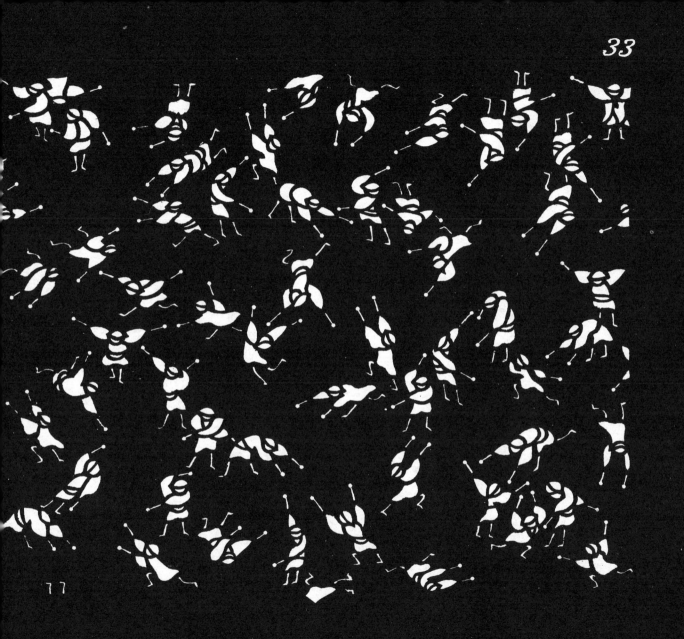

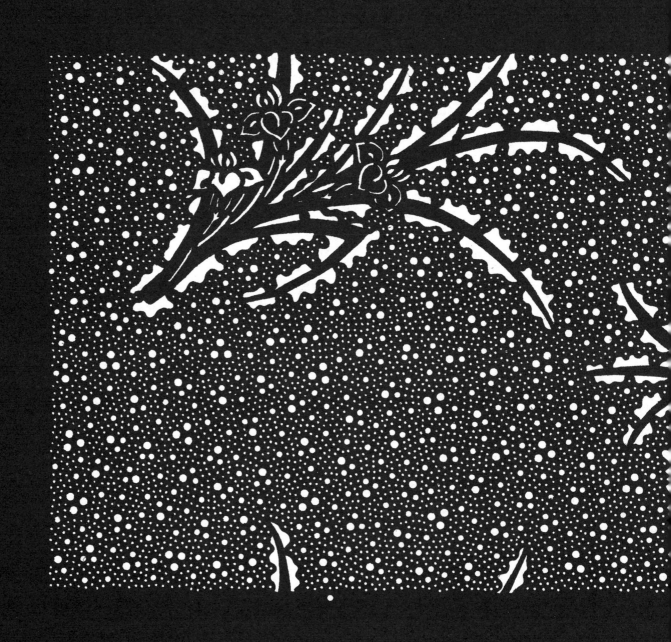

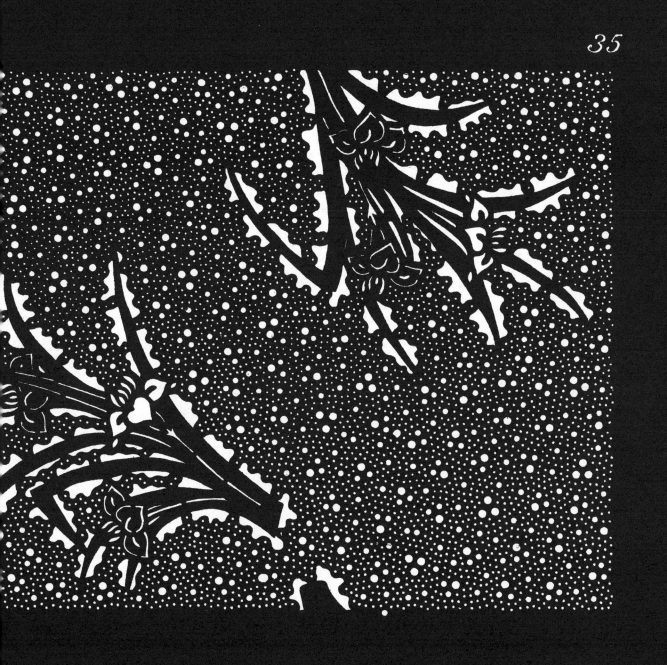

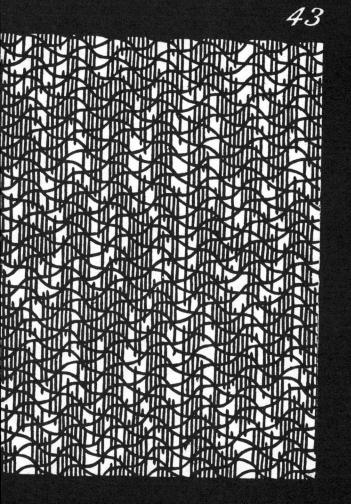

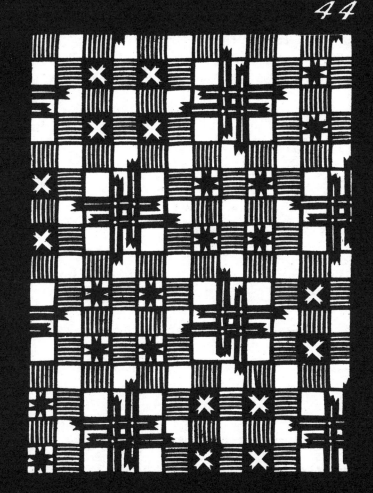

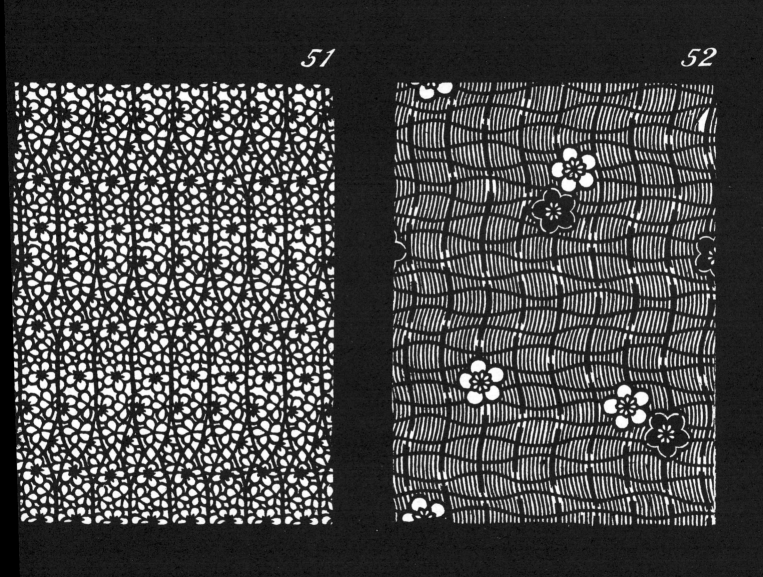

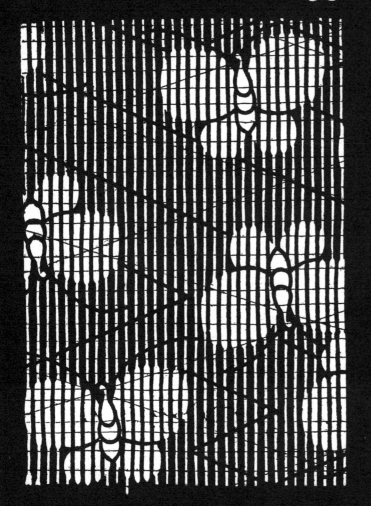

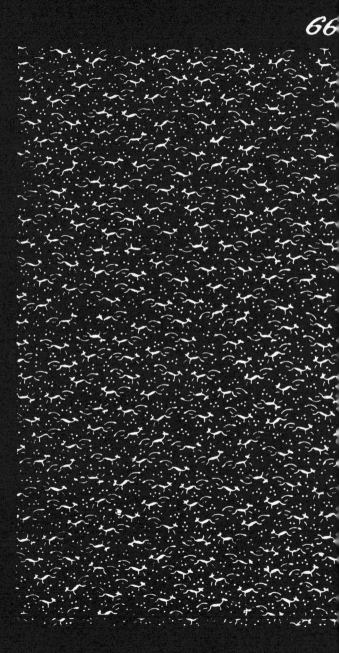

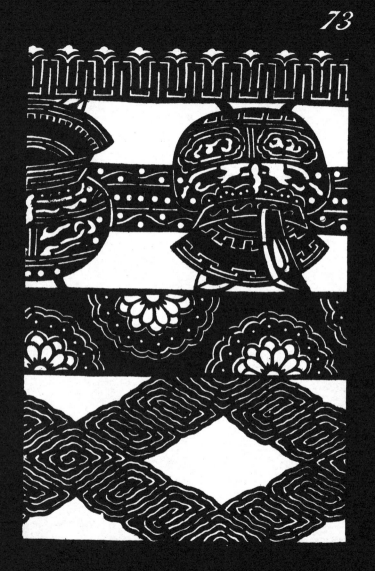

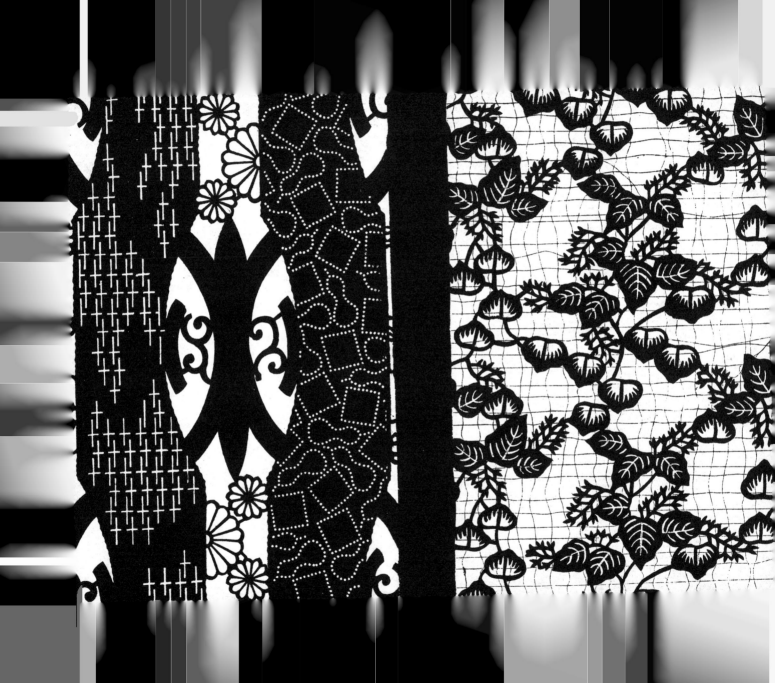

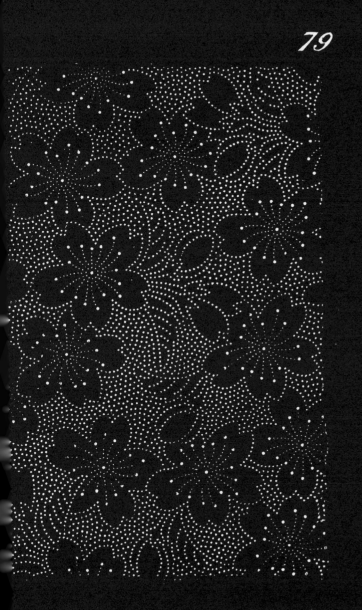

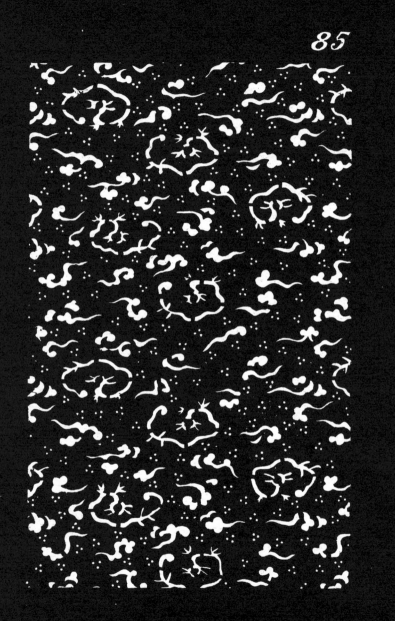

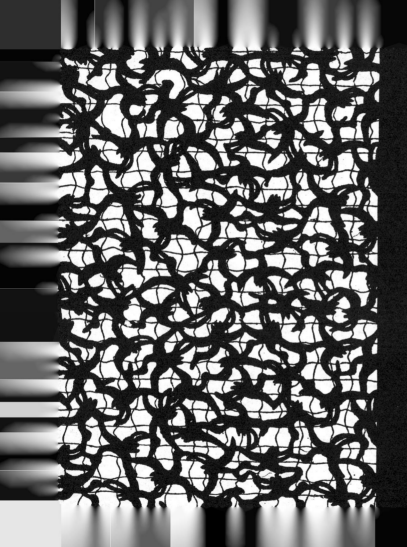

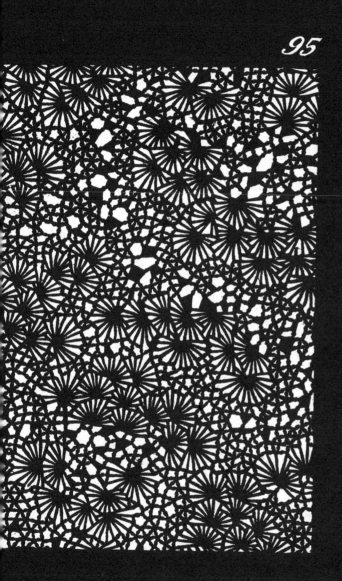

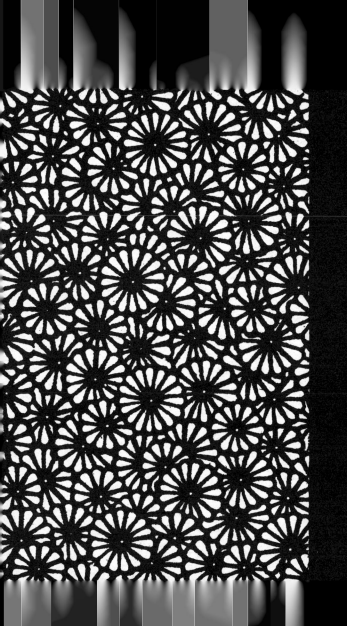

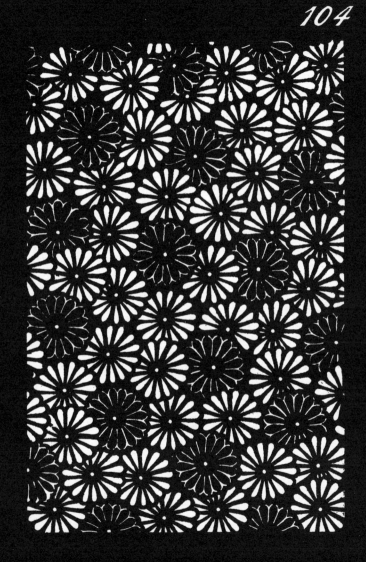